D1613462

JN-LINE

Mortimer's Fun with Words

Letters
Make Words

Karen Bryant-Mole

Gareth Stevens Publishing
A WORLD ALMANAC EDUCATION GROUP COMPANY

Mortimer's Fun with Words

For a free color catalog describing Gareth Stevens' list of high-quality books and multimedia programs, call 1-800-542-2595 (USA) or 1-800-461-9120 (Canada). Gareth Stevens Publishing's Fax: (414) 332-3567.

Library of Congress Cataloging-in-Publication Data available upon request from publisher.
Fax: (414) 332-3567 for the attention of the Publishing Records Department.

ISBN 0-8368-2748-1

This North American edition first published in 2000 by
Gareth Stevens Publishing
A World Almanac Education Group Company
330 West Olive Street, Suite 100
Milwaukee, WI 53212 USA

This edition © 2000 by Gareth Stevens, Inc. Original © BryantMole Books, 1999. First published in 1999 by Evans Brothers Limited, 2A Portman Mansions, Chiltern Street, London W1M 1LE, United Kingdom. Additional end matter © 2000 by Gareth Stevens, Inc.

Created by Karen Bryant-Mole
Photographs by Zul Mukhida
Designed by Jean Wheeler
Teddy bear by Merrythought Ltd.

Printed in the United States of America

1 2 3 4 5 6 7 8 9 04 03 02 01 00

contents

letters at the beginning

Mortimer is eating a bun.

The word **bun** begins with the letter **b**.

Can you find two words that
begin with the letter **b**?

bus

bag

car

Mortimer is playing with a toy jet.

The word **jet** begins with the letter **j**.

bat

Can you find another word that begins with the letter **j**?

jar

box

Mortimer is playing with a toy car.

The word **car** begins with the letter **c**.

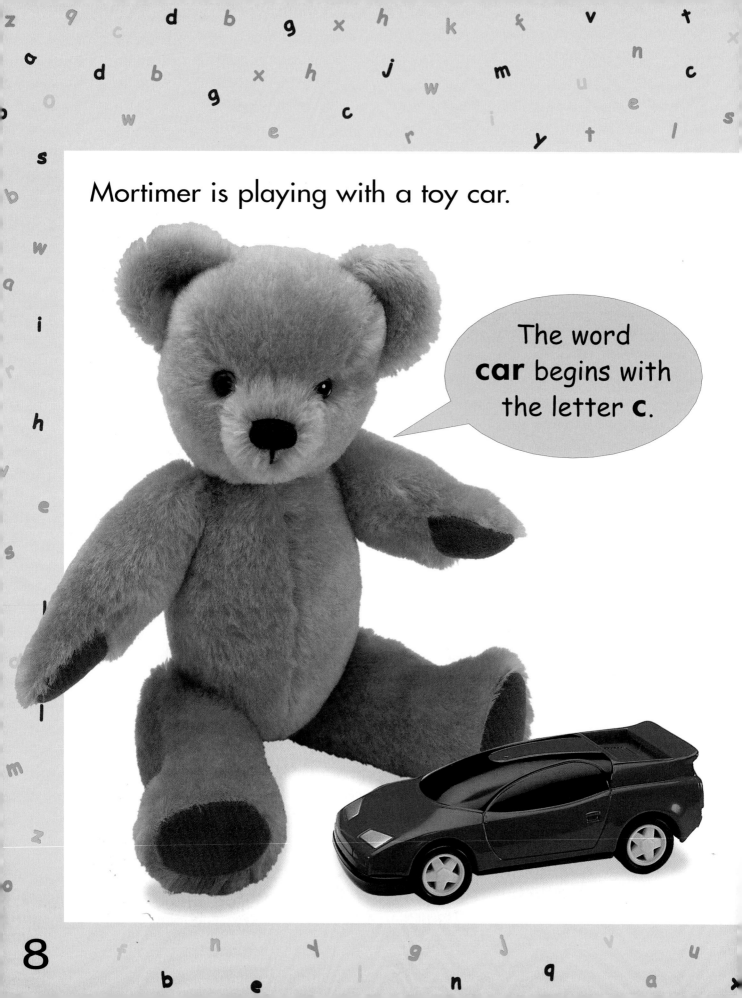

Can you find another word that begins with the letter **c**?

cup

bag

pig

The sun is shining on Mortimer.

The word **sun** ends with the letter **n**.

All these words end
with the letter **n**.

Can you name them?

pan

can

van

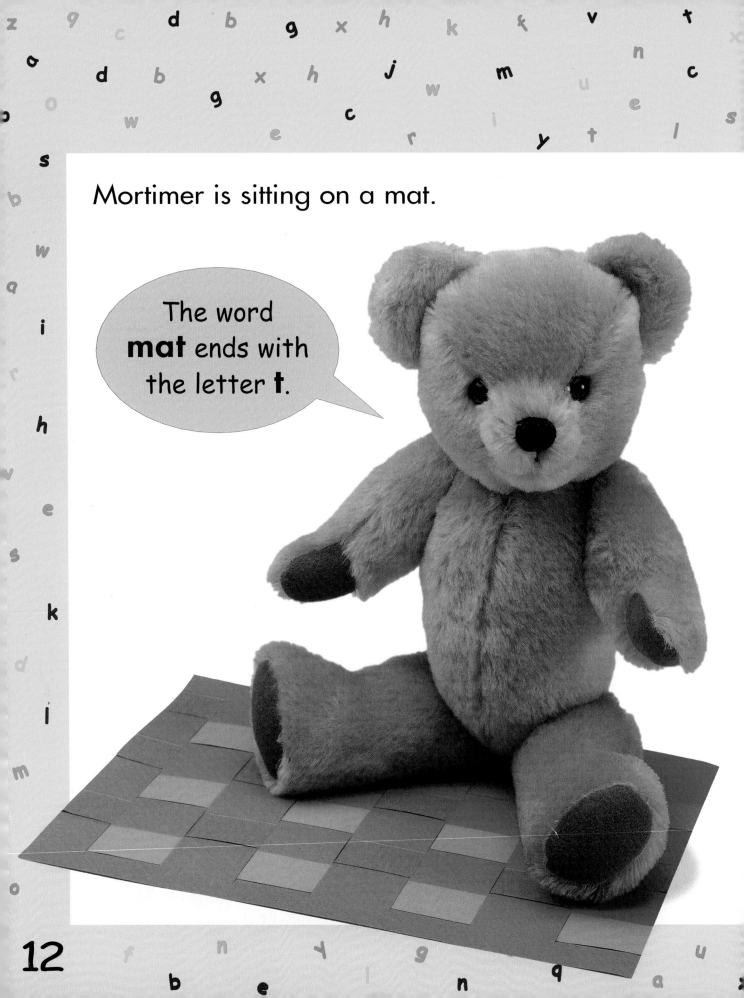

Mortimer is sitting on a mat.

The word **mat** ends with the letter **t**.

hat

Can you find another word
that ends with the letter **t**?

box

cup

13

Mortimer will use this red pot to cook dinner.

The word **pot** ends with the letter **t**.

Can you find another word
that ends with the letter **t**?

cat

can

bed

letters in the middle

Mortimer has a starfish in his net.

The word **net** has the letter **e** in the middle.

Can you find two more words
with the letter **e** in the middle?

hen

hat

pen

Mortimer caught a fish with his fishing rod.

The word **rod** has the letter **o** in the middle.

18

Can you find another word with the letter **o** in the middle?

dog

pan

hat

Mortimer is playing with six blocks.

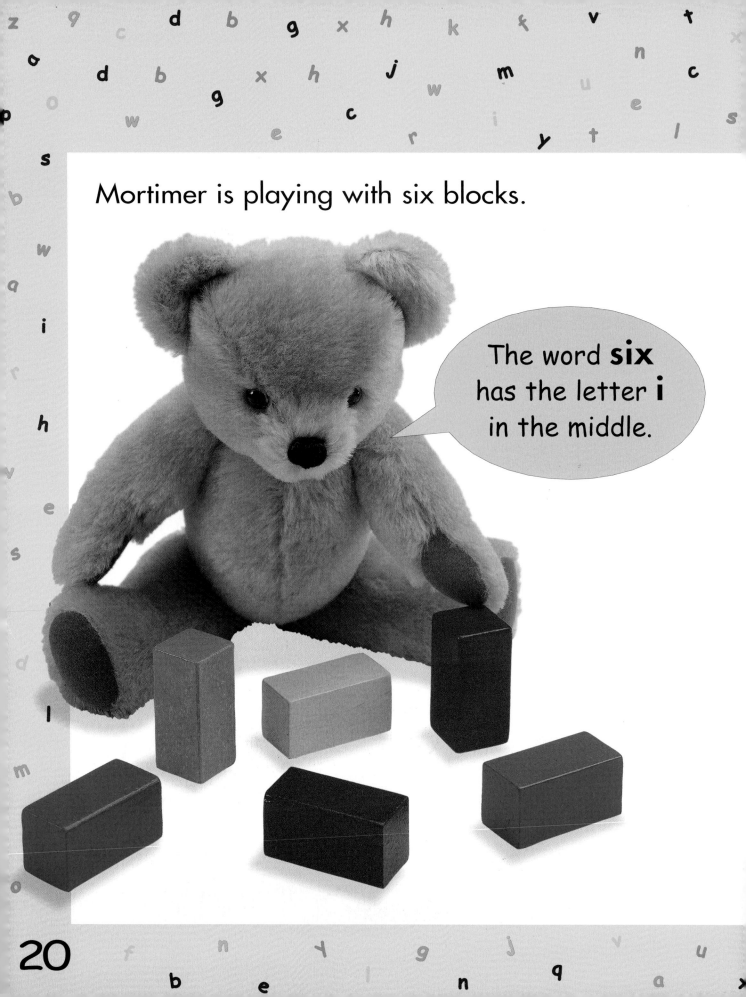

The word **six** has the letter **i** in the middle.

Can you find another word with the letter **i** in the middle?

pig

egg

van

letters make words

Mortimer has made a word with three letters.

The beginning letter is **c**, the end letter is **t**, and the middle letter is **a**.

Mortimer's letters make a word
that is the name of an animal.

Which animal is it?

glossary/index

bat — a furry, flying animal that sleeps during the day and comes out at night 7

bun — a type of soft bread with a round shape 4

fishing rod — a pole with a string and hook attached that is used to catch fish 18

hen — a grown-up female chicken 17

jet — a fast airplane that uses special engines to fly 6

mat — material that covers the floor like a small rug and is sometimes padded 12

net — fabric with many holes that is usually used to catch or hold something 16

starfish — a sea animal with a flat body and five arms that make the shape of a star 16

van — a big, box-shaped vehicle with a closed back end 11, 21

videos

Letter Fun. (Tapeworm)

Richard Scarry's Best ABC Video Ever! (Sony Wonder)

Sesame Street – Learning About Letters. (Sony Wonder)